© 2002 by Barbour Publishing, Inc.

ISBN 1-59310-892-3

All scripture quotations are taken from the King James Version of the Bible.

Cover image © Pictures Now
Cover and interior design by Karen Cassel Bear.

Published by Barbour Publishing, Inc., P.O. Box 719, Uhrichsville, Ohio 44683, www.barbourbooks.com

Our mission is to publish and distribute inspirational products offering exceptional value and biblical encouragement to the masses.

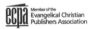 Member of the
Evangelical Christian
Publishers Association

Printed in China.
5 4 3 2 1

Season's Greetings

Rachel Quillin

DayMaker
GREETING BOOKS

May the Joy of
That First Christmas
Be Yours

I will honor Christmas in my heart
and try to keep it all the year.

Charles Dickens

Dear Jesus, thank You for coming to earth
that first Christmas. Thank You for the new
life and joy that we have because of Your
great love. Help us to eagerly share it
with others.

My soul doth magnify
the Lord,
And my spirit hath
rejoiced in God my Saviour.

Luke 1:46—47

Christ was born in the first century,
yet He belongs to all centuries.
He was born a Jew,
yet He belongs to all races.
He was born in Bethlehem,
yet He belongs to all countries.

George W. Truett

The universal joy of Christmas is certainly wonderful. We ring the bells when princes are born, or toll a mournful dirge when great men pass away. Nations have their red-letter days, their carnivals and festivals, but once a year and only once, the whole world stands still to celebrate the advent of a life. Only Jesus of Nazareth claims this worldwide, undying remembrance. You cannot cut Christmas out of the calendar nor out of the heart of the world.

Anonymous

Joy to the World

Joy to the world! the Lord is come!
Let earth receive her King;
Let every heart prepare Him room,
And heaven and nature sing,
And heaven and nature sing,
And heaven, and heaven, and nature sing.

Isaac Watts

When they saw the star,
they rejoiced with
exceeding great joy.

Matthew 2:10

Wishing You
God's Blessings
As You Celebrate
Our Savior's Birth

And, behold, thou shalt conceive in thy womb,
and bring forth a son, and shalt call his name JESUS.
He shall be great, and shall be called the Son of the Highest:
and the Lord God shall give unto him
the throne of his father David:
And he shall reign over the house of Jacob for ever;
and of his kingdom there shall be no end.

Luke 1:31–33

Take time to be aware that in the very midst of our busy preparations for the celebration of Christ's birth in ancient Bethlehem, Christ is reborn in the Bethlehems of our homes and daily lives. Take time, slow down, be still, be awake to the Divine Mystery that looks so common and so ordinary yet is wondrously present.

Edward Hays

The simple shepherds heard the voice of an angel
and found their Lamb;
the wise men saw the light of a star
and found their Wisdom.

Fulton J. Sheen

Blessed be the Lord God of Israel; for he hath
visited and redeemed his people, And hath
raised up an horn of salvation for us
in the house of his servant David.

Luke 1:68—69

At Christmastime...

people seem ready to stop and acknowledge the
blessings of God—more than at any other time
of the year. After all, this is the time we've set aside
to celebrate His greatest blessing to mankind—
the gift of His perfect, holy Son, Jesus Christ.
Only through Him can we truly enjoy the many
gifts that God bestows upon us. So, as we
celebrate this joyful season, let's take a moment;
let's reflect upon the many times that God has
blessed us this year. As we count our blessings,
we may be surprised and delighted to discover
that they are innumerable!

Praying You'll Be
Filled with God's
Peace and Love
During This
Special Season

Dear God,

Please be with my loved ones at this wonderful time. There is so much excitement, and there are so many things to do. It's easy to become overwhelmed by the hectic schedules that we place upon ourselves. Lord, please keep each friend and family member in your care. Give everyone the peace that we can know only through You. Help us all to relax so that we might fully experience the joy of Christmas. Thank You.

And the angel said unto them,
Fear not: for, behold,
I bring you good tidings of great joy,
which shall be to all people.
For unto you is born this day
in the city of David a Saviour,
which is Christ the Lord.

Luke 2:10—11

Glory to God in the highest,
and on earth peace,
good will toward men.

Luke 2:14

Somehow, not only at Christmas,
but all the long year through,
the joy that you give to others
is the joy that comes back to you.

John Greenleaf Whittier

God Bless You
Now and Always

And the angel came in unto her, and said,
Hail, thou that art highly favoured,
the Lord is with thee:
blessed art thou among women.

Luke 1:28

Christmas is based on an exchange of gifts:
the gift of God to man—His Son;
and the gift of man to God—
when we first give ourselves to God.

Anonymous

It was always said of him, that he knew
how to keep Christmas well, if any man alive
possessed the knowledge. May that be truly
said of us, and all of us! And so, as Tiny Tim
observed, "God Bless Us, Every One!"

Charles Dickens

God grant you the light in Christmas, which is faith;
the warmth of Christmas, which is love;
the radiance of Christmas, which is purity;
the righteousness of Christmas, which is justice;
the belief in Christmas, which is truth;
the all of Christmas, which is Christ.

Wilda English

Best of all, Christmas means a spirit of love, a time when the love of God and the love of our fellow men should prevail over all hatred and bitterness, a time when our thoughts and deeds and the spirit of our lives manifest the presence of God.

Anonymous

O Father, may that holy star
Grow every year more bright,
And send its glorious beams afar
To fill the world with light.

William Cullen Bryant

Are you willing to believe that love is
the strongest thing in the world—
stronger than hate, stronger than evil,
stronger than death—
and that the blessed life which began
in Bethlehem nineteen hundred years ago
is the image and brightness of the Eternal
    Love?
Then you can keep Christmas.

Henry Van Dyke

May You Enjoy
This Christmas
with Wonder and
Childlike Awe

Heap on more wood!—the wind is chill;
But let it whistle as it will,
We'll keep our Christmas merry still.

Sir Walter Scott

Suffer little children,

and forbid them not,

to come unto me:

for of such is the kingdom of heaven.

Matthew 19:14

Jingle Bells

Jingle bells, jingle bells,
jingle all the way!
O what fun it is to ride
In a one-horse open sleigh.

Dashing through the snow
In a one-horse open sleigh,
Over the fields we go,
Laughing all the way;
Bells on bob-tails ring,
Making spirits bright,
What fun it is to ride and sing
A sleighing song tonight.

Jingle bells, jingle bells,
jingle all the way!
O what fun it is to ride
In a one-horse open sleigh.

Happy, happy Christmas,
that can win us back to
the delusions of our childhood days,
recall to the old man the pleasures of his youth,
and transport the traveler back to
his own fireside and quiet home!

Charles Dickens

Moving between the legs of tables and of chairs, rising or falling, grasping at kisses and toys, advancing boldly, sudden to take alarm, retreating to the corner of arm and knee, eager to be reassured, taking pleasure in the fragrant brilliance of the Christmas tree.

T. S. Eliot

And they came with haste,

and found Mary, and Joseph,

and the babe lying in a manger.

And when they had seen it,

they made known abroad the saying

which was told them concerning this child.

And all they that heard it

wondered at those things

which were told them by the shepherds.

Luke 2:16—18

At Christmas
and Always,
May Your Heart
Rejoice in the
Gifts of God!

How Great Our Joy

While by the sheep we watched at night,
Glad tidings brought an angel bright.
There shall be born, so he did say,
In Bethlehem a Child today.
There shall the Child lie in a stall,
This Child who shall redeem us all.
This gift of God we'll cherish well,
That ever joy our hearts shall fill.
How great our joy! Great our joy!
Joy, joy, joy! Joy, joy, joy!
Praise we the Lord in heaven on high!
Praise we the Lord in heaven on high!

Translated by Theodore Baker

The rooms were very still while the pages were softly turned and the winter sunshine crept in to touch the bright heads and serious faces with a Christmas greeting.

Louisa May Alcott

It is Christmas in the mansion,
Yule-log fires and silken frocks;
It is Christmas in the cottage,
Mother's filling little socks.
It is Christmas on the highway,
In the thronging busy mart;
But the dearest, truest Christmas
Is the Christmas in the heart.

Anonymous

But the angel said unto him, Fear not, Zacharias: for thy prayer is heard; and thy wife Elisabeth shall bear thee a son, and thou shalt call his name John.

And thou shalt have joy and gladness; and many shall rejoice at his birth.

Luke 1:13–14

Dear Lord,

As Zacharias and Elisabeth rejoiced at the birth of their own son that first Christmas, may we also rejoice in Your many blessings to us. Thank You, God, for these blessings. Please help us to share them with others. Amen.

Reflective Joy

I feel the influence of the season beaming into my soul from the happy looks of those around me. Surely happiness is reflective like the light of heaven; and every countenance, bright with smiles and glowing with innocent enjoyment, is a mirror, transmitting to others the rays of a supreme and ever-shining benevolence.

Washington Irving

Then be ye glad, good people,
This night of all the year,
And light ye up your candles;
His star is shining near!

Author Unknown